Spiritual Warfare
Dr. Joffre P. Vivoni

Foundations Publishing
2010

Spiritual Warfare © 2009 by Dr. Joffre P. Vivoni
English Edition

All rights reserved including the right to reproduce, photocopy or to translate this book or any part thereof without prior permission of the copyright holder, except as provided by the copyright law.

ISBN O-9796940-8-6

Unless specified, all verses of the Bible are taken from the King James Version

Foundations Publishing
P.O. Box 8068
Jacksonville, FL 32239-8068
904-221-7606
www.biblefoundations.net

Dedication

I want to dedicate this book to my wife Elia and my children Jann, Eliane, and Laurita, who encouraged me to write it and above all, to my Lord Jesus for His inspiration.

I would also like to thank my wife Dr. Elia E. Vivoni for her arduous work in proofreading and editing and my son Jann Pascal Vivoni for his beautiful cover design.

I pray this book will be a blessing and a useful instrument in preparing you, the reader, for the abundant life in Christ. In the difficult times in which we live, we face so many struggles in our daily lives that we need to learn how to defend ourselves spiritually. It is easy to get distracted and fight in the flesh what we can only win in the Spirit.

Forward	1
Chapter One- Spiritual Warfare	3
Chapter Two- The Nature of Satan	7
Chapter Three- Satan's Control Center	17
Chapter Four- Satan's Battlefield	21
Chapter Five- Our Protection	27
Chapter Six- Preparing for Battle	37
Chapter Seven- Training for Battle	45
Chapter Eight- The Offensive	51
Chapter Nine- The Weapons We Need	55
Conclusion	62
About the Author	63

Foreword

It may seem uncommon to find a foreword written by the author's wife. I purposely asked my husband to allow me to do this for the simple fact that this book is a miracle in itself. I wish to give the Lord Jesus Christ the glory for what He has done in my husband's life and in our family because my husband suffered three strokes in September, 2007, which left him in a wheelchair and unable to see clearly, write, or type. He had the strokes just before starting to preach on the Sunday morning of September 9. He was taken by ambulance from our church to St. Luke's Hospital here in Jacksonville, where he spent five days in ICU. On September 15, he was transferred to Brooks Rehabilitation Hospital for therapy and came home on Oct. 3, 2007. He had uncontrollable hiccups which would affect him day and night. The doctors said his vocal cord on the right side was paralyzed. His lungs collapsed. The stroke affected his sense of balance, so besides not being able to walk and having to use a wheelchair, he had trouble with his sight. He could not focus at all - he saw multiple images of us. His hands would not obey commands. When he got a little better, he tried going to the computer but he could neither see the screen nor type.

The Lord has done an amazing work in my husband. Last year, as he began to improve, he started working on the publishing house. Although he had written <u>La Guerra Espiritual</u> in 2007 before the strokes, it was in a pamphlet form, so it has taken many hours of work for him to revise it, translate it, and get the manuscripts ready for printing. I give the Lord all the glory and the honor, because I know that without His help and intervention, this book and the others my husband is writing would not be possible. We understand that the Lord allowed my husband to live and allows him to improve daily because He still has a plan for his life. For that, we are grateful and we humbly acknowledge the Lord's mercy, favor, and kindness.

Dr. Elia E. Vivoni

CHAPTER 1
SPIRITUAL WARFARE

So shall they fear the name of the LORD from the west, and his glory from the rising of the sun. When the enemy shall come in like a flood, the Spirit of the LORD shall lift up a standard against him.
Isaiah 59:19

The purpose of this book is to bring awareness to the fact that we are fighting today the greatest and most difficult battle the body of Christ has ever encountered. This is not a physical battle between countries, but a spiritual battle between two kingdoms - the kingdom of God and the kingdom of Satan. If we do not get ready and fight the battle effectively, we can easily fall in the trap of the devil and be defeated by losing many of the blessings God has for us.

We can see below how the different translations of Ephesians 6:10-12 describe this battle:

King James Version-
Finally my brethren, be strong in the Lord, and in the power of his might. (11) Put on the whole armour of God, that ye may be able to stand against the wiles of the devil. (12) For we wrestle not against flesh and blood, but against principalities, against powers, against the rulers of the darkness of this world, against spiritual wickedness in high places.

New International Version-
Finally be strong in the Lord and in his mighty power. (11) Put on the full armor of God so that you can take your stand against the devil's schemes. (12) For our struggle is not against flesh and blood, but against the rulers, against the authorities, against the powers of this dark world and against the spiritual forces of evil in the heavenly realms.

Amplified Bible-
In conclusion, be strong in the Lord [be empowered through your union with Him]; draw your strength from Him [that strength which His boundless might provides]. (11) Put on God's whole armor [the armor of a heavy-armed soldier which God supplies], that you may be able successfully to stand up against [all] the strategies and the deceits of the devil. (12) For we are not wrestling with flesh and blood [contending only with physical opponents], but against the despotisms, against the powers, against [the master spirits who are] the world rulers of this present darkness, against the spirit forces of wickedness in the heavenly (supernatural) sphere.

Contemporary English Version-
Finally let the mighty strength of the Lord make you strong. (11) Put on all the armor that God gives, so you can defend yourself against the devil's tricks. (12) We are not fighting against humans. We are fighting against forces and authorities and against rulers of darkness and powers in the spiritual world.

Maybe you do not believe that Satan has a kingdom, but if the Bible teaches about it, we have to believe it. In Matthew 12: 22-28, our Lord Jesus speaks to us about this kingdom, especially in verses 23-25:

And all the people were amazed, and said, Is not this the son of David? (24) But when the Pharisees heard it, they said, This fellow doth not cast out devils, but by Beelzebub the prince of the devils. (25) And Jesus knew their thoughts, and said unto them, Every kingdom divided against itself is brought to desolation; and every city or house divided against itself shall not stand.

If we read carefully, we can learn the following things:

1. Satan is called Beelzebub or "Lord of the flies".

2. Satan has a kingdom and his kingdom is united and organized.

We must note, however, that Satan is not the only one who has a kingdom. There is another kingdom, the kingdom of God, and as stated in Colossians 1:12-14, all who serve God are soldiers of His kingdom.

Giving thanks unto the Father which hath made us meet to be partakers of the inheritance of the saints in light: (13) Who hath delivered us from the power of darkness, and hath translated us into the kingdom of his dear Son: (14) In whom we have redemption through his blood, even the forgiveness of sins.

Since we are in the latter days, the warfare between these two kingdoms has increased. Satan knows his time is getting short. Praise God, we also know Who has won the battle, our Commander-in-chief, Jesus. In order to secure the victory, we have to do what the Bible teaches us in James 4:7:

Submit yourselves therefore to God. Resist the devil, and he will flee from you.

CHAPTER 2
THE NATURE OF SATAN
WHO IS SATAN? WHO ARE THE MEMBERS OF HIS KINGDOM?

How art thou fallen from heaven, O Lucifer son of the morning! How art thou cut down to the ground, which didst weaken the nations! For thou hast said in thine heart, I will ascend into heaven, I will exalt my throne above the stars of God: I will sit also upon the mount of the congregation, in the sides of the north.
Isaiah 14:12-14

We have established through the Word that there are two kingdoms, the kingdom of God and the kingdom of Satan. Several years ago, when somebody mentioned Satan, people would laugh. They did not give him much importance and many thought he was the product of the imagination of religious fanatics or an entity that had no influence on this earth. Even today, with so many crimes related to Satanic cults, many people still insist that Satan is not real, and thus, he is working freely with hardly any resistance from believers. He therefore influences greatly the behavior of many people.

Who is Satan?
It is important to know that Satan is not a product of any person's imagination. He is neither an idea nor an influence; he is real. He is not a human being; he is a spiritual being. The Bible speaks about him and mentions his titles and names in Revelations 20:2:

And he laid hold on the dragon, that old serpent which is the Devil, and Satan, and bound him a thousand years.

In Isaiah 14:12-15, the Bible speaks about his attributes and actions:

How art thou fallen from heaven, O Lucifer son of the morning! How art thou cut down to the ground, which didst weaken the nations! (13) For thou hast said in thine heart, I will ascend into heaven, I will exalt my throne above the stars of God: I will sit also upon the mount of the congregation, in the sides of the north: I will ascend above the heights of the clouds; I will be like the most High. (15) Yet thou shalt be brought down to hell, to the sides of the pit.

For this reason, Jesus treated him as an individual and fought him as such. Matthew 4: 1-11 tells us that Jesus was tempted by Satan and shows us how He fought back.

Then was Jesus led up of the Spirit into the wilderness to be tempted of the devil. (2) And when he had fasted forty days and forty nights, he was afterward an hungred. (3) And when the tempter came to him, he said, If thou be the Son of God, command that these stones be made bread. (4) But he answered and said It is written, Man shall not live by bread alone, but by every word that proceedeth out of the mouth of God. (5) Then the devil taketh him up into the holy city and setteth him on a pinnacle of the temple, (6) And saith unto him, If thou be the Son of God, cast thyself down: for it is written, He shall give his angels charge concerning thee: and in their hands they shall bear thee up, lest at any time thou dash thy foot against a stone. (7) Jesus said unto him, It is written again, Thou shalt not tempt the Lord thy God. (8) Again, the devil taketh him up into an exceeding high mountain, and sheweth him all the kingdoms of the world, and the glory of them; (9) And saith unto him, All these things will I give thee, if thou wilt fall down and worship me. (10) Then saith Jesus unto him, Get thee hence, Satan: for it is written, Thou shall worship the Lord thy God, and him only shall thou serve. (11) Then the devil leaveth him, and, behold, angels came and ministered unto him.

Ephesians 6:10-18 warns us in this manner:

Finally my brethren, be strong in the Lord, and in the power of his might! (11) Put on the whole armour of God, that ye may be able to stand against the wiles of the devil. (12) For we wrestle not against flesh and blood but against principalities, against powers, against the rulers of the darkness of this world, against spiritual wickedness in high places. (13) Wherefore take unto you the whole armour of God, that ye may be able to withstand in the evil day, and having done all, to stand. (14) Stand therefore, having your loins girt about with truth, and having on the breastplate of righteousness; (15) And your feet shod with the preparation of the gospel of peace; (16) Above all, taking the shield of faith, wherewith ye shall be able to quench all the fiery darts of the wicked.

(17) And take the helmet of salvation, and the sword of the Spirit, which is the word of God: (18) Praying always with all prayer and supplication in the Spirit, and watching thereunto with all perseverance and supplication for all the saints.

As I previously stated, we have a real enemy, an individual who wants to destroy us and against whom we have to fight. This enemy is Satan.

Where does Satan come from?
The Bible tells us that God created Satan; however, God did not create him the way he is today. In Ezekiel 28:12-19, we read that God created Satan as a beautiful being. Let us read his description:

Son of man, take up a lamentation upon the king of Tyrus, and say unto him, Thus saith the Lord GOD; Thou sealest up the sum, full of wisdom, and perfect in beauty. (13) Thou hast been in Eden the garden of God; every precious stone was thy covering, the sardius, topaz, and the diamond, the beryl, the onyx, and the jasper, the sapphire, the emerald, and the carbuncle, and gold: the workmanship of thy tabrets and of thy pipes was prepared in thee in the day that thou wast created. (14) Thou art the anointed cherub that covereth; and I have set thee so: thou wast upon the holy mountain of God; thou hast walked up and down in the midst of the stones of fire. (15)Thou wast perfect in thy ways from the day that thou wast created, till iniquity was found in thee. (16) By the multitude of thy merchandise they have filled the midst of thee with violence, and thou hast sinned: therefore I will cast thee as profane out of the mountain of God:

and I will destroy thee, O covering cherub, from the midst of the stones of fire. (17) Thine heart was lifted up because of thy beauty, thou hast corrupted thy wisdom by reason of thy brightness: I will cast thee to the ground, I will lay thee before kings, that they may behold thee. (18) Thou hast defiled thy sanctuaries by the multitude of thine iniquities, by the iniquity of thy traffick; therefore will I bring forth a fire from the midst of thee, it shall devour thee, and I will bring thee to ashes upon the earth in the sight of all them that behold thee. (19) All they that know thee among the people shall be astonished at thee: thou shalt be a terror: and never shalt thou be any more.

We read in verse 12 that Satan was described as *"full of wisdom and perfect in beauty"*. He had a high rank in heaven, as implied by the way he is described in verse 13, and in heaven, he was involved in the ministry of worship. In verses 14 and 15, he is described this way:

Thou art the anointed cherub that covereth, and I have set thee so: thou wast upon the holy mountain of God; thou hast walked up and down in the midst of the stones of fire, (15), thou wast perfect in thy ways from the day that thou wast created.

All this lasted, however, until "iniquity was found" in him. Satan's sin was that he exalted himself and wanted to be equal to God (verse17). As a result, he was cast out of heaven. The fall of Satan is also described in Isaiah 14:12-15.

(12) How art thou fallen from heaven, O Lucifer son of the morning! How art thou cut down to the ground, which didst weaken the nations! (13) For thou hast said in thine heart, I will ascend into heaven, I will exalt my throne above the stars of God: I will sit also upon the mount of the congregation, in the sides of the north: (14) I will ascend above the heights of the clouds; I will be like the most High. (15) Yet thou shalt be brought down to hell, to the sides of the pit.

From that time on, the most common weapons that Satan uses are pride and ambition.

Who are the demons?

Theories from very well-known personalities in the Christian realm try to answer this question. Unfortunately, many of these theories are based on conclusions they have reached by playing with words and by having big imaginations. For example, there is a theory that says that demons are re-encarnations of pre-adamic beings.

People who believe in this theory affirm that between Genesis 1:1 and 1:2, millions of years passed, and that during this period of time a big spiritual battle caused the earth to be void and without form. They affirm that these beings that inhabited the earth during that period became the demons that we know today. According to these people, this is why God, after blessing Adam & Eve, said to them in Genesis 1:28:

Be fruitful, and multiply and replenish the earth, and subdue it: and have dominion over the fish of the sea, and over the fowl of the land and over every living thing that moveth upon the earth.

The word "replenish ("male" (maw-lay)}" can be translated in at least two ways: one is "to fill" and the other is "to refill". These people prefer the translation that suggests God was telling them to refill the earth; so, if they were to refill it, it would be logical to say that there was a pre-adamic race that lived and filled the earth before Adam and Eve. I would rather limit myself to what the Bible states, not to any conclusions that I may think of; that way, I can be sure that I am stating the Word and not my interpretation or my imagination.

Matthew 25:41 speaks about *"the everlasting fire prepared for the devil and his angels".* Revelations 12:4 tells us about the dragon (the devil) that drew the third part of the stars of heaven with his tail and cast them to the earth.

And his tail drew the third part of the stars of heaven, and did cast them to the earth: and the dragon stood before the woman which was ready to be delivered, for to devour her child as soon as it was born.

Many experts agree that the term "stars" in this verse refers to angels. In other words, the devil (Satan) took a third of the angels with him.

Revelations 12: 9 verifies our assumption.

And the great dragon was cast out, that old serpent, called the Devil, and Satan, which deceiveth the whole world:

he was cast out into the earth, and his angels were cast out with him.

As we can see, the demons are those fallen angels or evil spirits that the Bible refers to in these verses. The term "demon" comes from the Latin word "doemon" that means "evil spirit" and from the Greek word "daimon" that means "divine being".

There are a few things I wish to point out abut demons:

1. Demons never die, so they have been on earth since the fall.

2. The demons are angry against God and have made it their priority to destroy everything and everyone that God loves or created, primarily mankind.

3. Demons are very organized.

4. Demons, like Satan, do not have a body like ours. Since they are spirits, they need a body in which they can manifest themselves. For this reason, they try to inhabit any person that allows himself to be possessed. Demons sometimes use the name of the person they inhabit.

5. Demons use nicknames. We see this in Mark 5:9 where the demon who was in the Gadarene called himself "Legion" because they were "many".

6. Demons are liars, so we cannot trust them. John 8:44 clearly states:

   When he speaketh a lie, he speaketh of his own: for he is a liar, and the father of it.

7. Some demons are more wicked than others. We see this in Matthew 12:45:

   Then goeth he, and taketh with himself seven other spirits more wicked than himself and they enter and dwell there: and the last state of that man is worst than the first. Even so shall it be also unto this wicked generation.

8. They also vary in power, as we can see in Mark 9:29:

   And he said unto them, This kind can come forth by nothing, but by prayer and fasting.

9. They know who has the power and authority to rebuke them. We see this in Acts 19:15:

   And the evil spirit answered and said, Jesus I know and Paul I know; but who are ye?

10. They are not spirits of dead people. They are fallen angels.

11. They believe in God and tremble (James 2:9). I want to point out that this belief in God is not based upon faith or trust and dedication to Him, but upon the knowledge that God is real and that they have only a short time left before they are punished.

12. Demons also have free will. Matthew 12:44 tells us this in relation to demons:

   Then he saith, I will return into my house from whence I came out; and when he is come, he findeth it empty, swept, and garnished.

We can continue saying that they oppose the people of God, the Believers. They have their own doctrines, as written in 1 Timothy 4:1:

Now the Spirit speaketh expressly, that in the latter times some shall depart from the faith, giving heed to seducing spirits, and doctrines of devils.

Having said that, the most important thing we should know is that they must be submitted to the authority and sovereignty of our Lord Jesus Christ, who, according to 1 Peter 3:22, is at the right hand of God, the angels and authorities and powers being made subject unto Him.

CHAPTER 3
SATAN'S CONTROL CENTER

I knew a man in Christ above fourteen years ago, (whether in the body I cannot tell; or whether out of the body I cannot tell: God knoweth;) such an one caught up to the third heaven.
2 Corinthians 12:2

Let us try to study where Satan's kingdom or control center is located. Reading Ephesians 6: 12, we see the following:

For we wrestle not against flesh and blood, but against principalities, against powers, against the rulers of the darkness of this world, against spiritual wickedness in high places.

From this verse we can say that Satan's kingdom is in "high places" (epouranios), which is also translated as "celestial places".

If God is in heaven and Satan's kingdom is in celestial places, how can we explain this? Genesis 1:1 states the following: *In the beginning God created the heavens* (shamayim) *and the earth.* The suffix "im" makes the word plural. The translation means that there is more than one heaven.

How many heavens do we have then?

Let us analyze this. There is one heaven that is easily seen and it is the location of the sun, the moon, and the stars.

We can easily say that this is the first heaven. On the other hand, in 2 Corinthians 12: 2-4, we read about the third heaven where God is. Let us read Ephesians 4:10:

> *He that descended is the same also that ascended up far above all heavens, that he might fill all things.*

If we have a first heaven and a third heaven, we can conclude that there are at least three heavens. What about the second heaven? Where is it? To understand more about the second heaven, let us read Daniel 10:12-14:

> *Then said he unto me, Fear not, Daniel: for from the first day that thou didst set thine heart to understand, and to chasten thyself before thy God, thy words were heard, and I am come for thy words. (13) But the prince of the kingdom of Persia withstood me one and twenty days: but, lo, Michael, one of the chief princes, came to help me; and I remained there with the kings of Persia. (14) Now I am come to make thee understand what shall befall thy people in the latter days: for yet the vision is for many days.*

We see that in this battle Satan was trying to prevent the message from reaching Daniel. He tried to prevent the messenger from accomplishing his mission by intercepting him while he was on his way to Daniel. We can conclude then that this attack was fought between the third heaven and the first heaven, or in other words, in the second heaven. We could then say that Satan is in the second heaven.

I want to point out that from these verses we can learn several things:

1. God heard Daniel's prayer from the first day and Satan could not prevent the answer from being sent. Definitely, Satan cannot prevent our prayers from reaching God, nor can he prevent God from answering our prayers.

2. In these passages we also read the term, "prince of Persia" implying that there are principalities assigned to different nations. Persia was one of the empires that dominated Israel during the period of 500 B.C.

If we continue reading the Bible, we see that there are some verses in the Scripture that imply that Satan still has access to the third heaven. A good example is Job 1:6-7 which reads like this:

Now there was a day when the sons of God came to present themselves before the LORD, and Satan came also among them. (7) And the LORD said unto Satan, Whence comest thou? Then Satan answered the LORD, and said, From going to and fro in the earth, and from walking up and down in it.

Job 2:1-2 is a very similar verse.

Why is it then that God still allows Satan to be in His presence?

The last part of Revelations 12:10 gives us an answer to this question:

And I heard a loud voice saying in heaven, Now is come salvation, and strength, and the kingdom of our God, and the power of his Christ: for the accuser of our brethren is cast down, which accused them before our God day and night.

The last part of this verse explains it by saying that Satan is the accuser of the brethren. The good thing about it is that it does not end there. It continues to say in Revelations 10:11,12:

And they overcame him by the blood of the Lamb, and by the word of their testimony; and they loved not their lives unto the death. (12) Therefore rejoice, ye heavens, and ye that dwell in them. Woe to the inhabiters of the earth and of the sea, for the devil is come down unto you, having great wrath, because he knoweth that he hath but a short time.

Hallelujah! The Lord will prevail and the enemy will one day torment God's people no more.

CHAPTER 4
SATAN'S BATTLEFIELD

For though we walk in the flesh, we do not war after the flesh: (4) (For the weapons of our warfare are not carnal, but mighty through God to the pulling down of strongholds;) (5) Casting down imaginations, and every high thing that exalts itself against the knowledge of God, and bringing into captivity every thought to the obedience of Christ;
2 Corinthians 10:3-5

Satan's main target is our mind. He tries to infiltrate ideas and temptations into our minds so that we would fall from the grace of God. If we fall, he can take us into captivity. If he succeeds in controlling our mind, he has almost won the battle. I say "almost won the battle," because with the help of God, we can always defeat him.

In 2 Corinthians 4:4, the Bible teaches us the following:

In whom the god of this world hath blinded the minds of them which believe not, lest the light of the glorious gospel of Christ, who is the image of God, should shine unto them.

Reading this verse we can see that Satan can build fortresses in the minds of human beings. A fortress is something that blinds our intelect so that the light of Jesus cannot penetrate. When this happens, the only way to be delivered and destroy those fortresses is by using spiritual weapons (2 Corinthians 10:3-5). Unfortunately, on many occasions we fight with carnal weapons against the people that oftend us. We do not realize that the enemy is behind the problem and that we have to fight against him, not against our brother or sister. We must use spiritual weapons to fight Satan. Remember, our victory does not depend on our physical strength. It depends on our relationship with God through Jesus.

Some of the fortresses that exist in the minds of human beings are things such as prejudices, pre-conceived ideas, erroneous ideas about God, political ideologies, racism, and fanatism. We as Christians have the power of the Holy Spirit to destroy any stronghold or fortress that occupies or is trying to occupy our mind. Satan, of course, does not want us to know the reality that Christ has already defeated him totally and forever. Jesus has not only defeated Satan, He has defeated all of Satan's principalities and powers. Christ defeated Satan at Calvary. Colossians 2:13-15 confirms it in this way:

And you, being dead in your sins and the uncircumcision of your flesh, hath he quickened together with him, having forgiven you all trespasses; (14) Blotting out the handwriting of ordinances that was against us, which was contrary to us, and took it out of the way nailing it to his cross; (15) And having spoiled principalities and powers, he made a shew of them openly triumphing over them in it.

We can learn three things from the previous verses:

a. The handwriting af ordinances is the law of Moses. Jesus took away the law as a requirement for righteousness. Now our faith is counted as righteousness.

b. Satan is the accuser, but God can and is willing to forgive us because Jesus paid the price at the cross.

c. Satan has no more right to accuse us because at the cross Jesus took away his greatest weapon and soon he will lose his position as an accuser. Revelation 12:10:

For the accuser of our brethren is cast down, which accused them before our God day and night.

When Satan comes to us and tries to accuse us because of our past, we should remind him of what is written in 2 Corinthians 5: 21:

For he hath made him to be sin for us, who knew no sin; that we might be made the righteousness of God in him.

In other words, Jesus, who never sinned, was made sin so that through His righteousness we may be righteous. This is the basis for our victory.

It is important to note that overcoming does not mean just winning a battle. It entails winning the war. Jesus obtained His victory against the Satanic world. Jesus won the victory for us. Now He wants us to make that victory known. 2 Corinthians 2:14:

Now thanks be unto God, which always causes us to triumph in Christ, and makes manifest the savour of his knowledge by us in every place.

Matthew 28:18-20 states:

And Jesus came and spake unto them, saying, All power is given unto me in heaven and in earth. (19) Go ye therefore, and teach all nations, baptizing them in the name of the Father and of the Son, and of the Holy Ghost: (20) Teaching them to observe all things whatsoever I have commanded you: and, lo, I am with you always, even unto the end of the world. Amen.

In other words, Jesus is saying to us, "I have the power, I have defeated Satan. Now you go and tell the world about my victory, and fulfill the command that I have given you."

Through His life, death, and resurrection, Jesus showed us that He overcame Satan. Here are several important events that illustrate this:

1. In the desert, Jesus defeated Satan when He resisted temptation after having fasted for 40 days.

2. In Gethsemane, He submitted to His father's will.

3. On Calvary, He obtained the victory for us at the cross by taking away our sins.

4. By His resurrection three days later, Jesus defeated death and fear.

We now have the responsibility to tell the world about our victory in Jesus. 2 Corinthians 2:14 says it clearly:

Now thanks be unto God, which always causes us to triumph in Christ, and maketh manifest the savour of his knowledge by us in every place.

I want to point out that, even though we definitely have the victory over the enemy, he will continually attack us in our minds trying to make us believe that he is in control and that we are defeated. It is for this reason that we need to resist until the end by using our spiritual weapons and staying firm in our relationship with God.

James 4:7 reassures us of our victory:

Submit yourselves therefore to God. Resist the devil, and he will flee from you.

In other words, the devil will try to tempt us continuously. We need to resist him and hold firm to the Word of God. The result is that he will flee from us.

CHAPTER 5
OUR PROTECTION
(THE ARMOR OF GOD)

Put on the whole armor of God, that ye may be able to stand against the wiles of the devil.
Ephesians 6:11

In ancient times, no king or general would go out for battle without the knowledge that his army was properly armed and protected. Not being properly armed or protected meant you would be defeated before you even started to fight. Once the soldiers received their armor and weaponry, they would begin training for battle. Paul, in the Epistle to the Ephesians, speaks to us about the armor of God, indicating the reality of the spiritual battle that we are facing. He also lets us know that we need to protect ourselves by using the whole armor so that we will not to be wounded in this spiritual battle.

Six parts make up the armor of God: the belt of truth, the breastplate of righteousness, your feet fitted with the readiness that comes from gospel of peace, the shield of faith, the helmet of salvation, and the sword of the Spirit.

Let us examine each part individually:

1. The belt of truth: In order for a Roman soldier to be able to fight comfortably, he needed to adjust his belt properly so that his tunic or skirt would not interfere with his movements. In battle it is of utmost importance that each soldier be able to move freely. For us as Christians, the belt is knowing the truth which is Jesus and walking always in that truth. It is not about knowing Jesus as someone who simply existed and whose teachings we need to follow. It is to know Him as our personal Savior and Lord, the Almighty, the King of kings and Lord of lords. It is to honor God and live by His Word daily, by being honest, sincere, and truthful. Lack of honesty and sincerity can be compared to a uniform that does not fit; it interferes with the soldier's ability to fight. For this reason, we need to always speak the truth. If we do, we will be able to please God and we will not have anything that interferes with our doing His perfect will. We must, however, tell the truth in love. I say this because there are people who say the truth in a manner that offends and hurts others. We need to follow what the Word says in Ephesians 4:15:

> *But speaking the truth in love, (that we) may grow up into him in all things, which is the head, even Christ.*

2. The breastplate of righteousness: The breastplate protecs the vital organs of the body, especially the heart. Proverbs 4:23 tells us: *Keep thy heart with all diligence; for out of it are the issues of life.* Paraphrasing, we would say, "Guard your heart with all of your strength; because all things in life come from it." What a person has in his/her heart will determine the path that the person will follow, whether good or bad. How can we be made righteous? How can we carry the breastplate of righteousness? To be righteous is to conform to God's moral and ethical standards. We as sinners are far from His standards. Only God can make us righteous. The Bible teaches us in 2 Corinthians 5:21:

For he hath made him to be sin for us, who knew no sin; that we might be made the righteousness of God in him.

In other words, only through Christ can we be acceptable to God. Here we come across a term which we need to define in order to understand our battle better and use our armor more efficiently, the term "justification." What is justification? Justification is an act of God in which a sinner is declared righteous in the eyes of God. This is something that only occurs through the redeeming work of Jesus. Due to our sinful nature, we deserve punishment. In order to be fair, God would have had to punish us. But God showed His love for us when He made His justice in Christ. You see, Jesus, even though He never sinned, received the chastisement and judgement of God for our sins upon Himself. By doing so, Christ paid the price and bought us with His blood so we would not have to be punished. This means that when we receive Christ as our personal Savior, we are justified or made acceptable to God by our faith in Him. Ephesians 2:8 (Contemporary English Version) says the following:

You were saved by faith in God who treats us much better than we deserve.

This is God's gift for you and not anything you have done on your own.

Other verses such as Philippians 3:9 (Contemporary English Version) speak to us in a similar way:

. . . and to know that I belong to him. I could not make myself acceptable to God by obeying the Law of Moses.

I understand, then, that God accepted me simply because of my faith in Christ.

We can only have the breastplate of righteousness when we put our faith in Jesus who justifies us. Therefore, when the devil accuses us, we can remind him that Jesus is the one who made us righteous.

3. **Your feet fitted with the readiness that comes from the gospel of peace:** This is a reference to the shoes that the legionnaires wore. They used heavy, open sandals that were fastened to their calves with leather straps, These sandals allowed the soldiers to march for long distances and to move fast when they received orders from their commander. We as Christians have to study and memorize Scriptures in order to teach the Gospel of Jesus appropriately. This is a Gospel that produces peace in the hearts and minds of those who believe. As it is written in John 14:27 (Contemporary English Version):

*I give you peace, the kind of peace that only I can give.
It isn't like the peace that this world can give. So do not be
worried or afraid.*

We need to have that peace in our hearts and minds in order to be able to transmit it when we preach the Gospel. Matthew 10:12-13 (Contemporary English Version) says this:

*When you go to a home, give it your blessing of peace. (13)
If the home is deserving, let your blessing remain with them.
But if the home isn't deserving, take back your blessing
of peace.*

This verse implies that nobody can give something they do not possess. To have our feet fitted with the readiness that comes from the gospel of peace means to know the Gospel, to have that peace that only God can give, and to be ready to act when God tells us to act. This also means taking the message of God to others.

4. The shield of faith: The ancient Romans used two types of shields. One was circular and small, used when the soldier was fighting by himself and needed mobility. The other shield was a long and rectangular shield (the thureos) from where the word "door" comes. This latter shield is the one referred to in this verse. The Roman soldiers would form human walls as they marched in unity, side by side, keeping their shields in front of them. Each soldier was responsible for covering the soldiers on each side of him and the back of the soldier in front of him. By doing this, the soldiers formed a solid wall that was almost impenetrable. Each soldier was trained never to break the wall. This way, if they were attacked, they did not have to worry about who was going to cover their back, since there was always someone to go to their defense. I want to express that on our own, it is extremely difficult to fight against the enemy. That is why it is of utmost importance for us to congregate and find our place in the body of Christ (the church). It is also important to join forces and form a strong wall for our defense. We need to become part of a congregation and create friendships with mature persons in the Lord, people who would help strengthen our faith and help us grow in the knowledge of the Word. This is how we can create a shield against the plans and weapons of the devil. Hebrews 11:1 teaches us the definition of faith.

Now faith is the substance of things hoped for, the evidence of things not seen.

Romans 10:17 adds:

So then faith cometh by hearing, and hearing by the word of God.

If we learn to use the Word as a shield, if we trust in the Lord and use His Word to cover and direct us, you can be assured that there will be no weapon that can penetrate and harm us.

5. The helmet of salvation: The helmet was the part of the armor that protected the soldier's head. Satan's battleground is our minds, so if we know that we are saved and that the promises of God are for us, this knowledge will help us to stay firm and to continue moving forward in our spiritual battle. Daily, we face many pressures and trials, especially if we are in ministry. One of the most powerful weapons used against us by the devil is depression. He uses depression to distract us and discourage us by making us believe that we are worthless and unable to fight for the Lord. Praise God that the Bible also gives us weapons to fight depression. Isaiah 61:3 says the following:

To appoint unto them that mourn in Zion, to give unto them beauty for ashes, the oil of joy for mourning, the garment of praise for the spirit of heaviness; that they might be called trees of righteousness, the planting of the LORD, that he might be glorified.

The spirit of heaviness is the same as depression.

Besides depression, the enemy uses negative thoughts, inferitority complexes, predjudice, and similar things. In His Word, however, God provides all of the weapons we need for our defense. Romans 8:37 (New International Version) says it clearly:

No, in all these things we are more than conquerors through him who loved us.

Below are other verses in the Bible that will help us win the battle:

1 Thessalonians 5:8 (Contemporary English Version):

But we belong to the day. So we must stay sober and let our faith and love be like a suit of armor. Our firm hope that we will be saved is our helmet.

Our faith in Jesus provides for our salvation. It commands us to love our neighbors. On the other hand, the knowledge of being saved protects our minds because we are aware of all the blessings God has for us. This hope is based upon the expectation that all of the promises of God are real and that no matter what we are going through, everything will be fine. In other words, it will allow us to see things through another perspective and help us fight depression.

Romans 8:28:

> *And we know that all things work together for good to them that love God, to them who are called according to his purpose.*

Hebrews 6:17-20 (Contemporary English Version):

> *So when God wanted to prove for certain that His promise to His people could not be broken, He made a vow. (18) God cannot tell lies! And so His promises and vows are two things that can never be changed. We have run to God for safety. Now His promises should greatly encourage us to take hold of the hope that is right in front of us. (19) This hope is like a firm and steady anchor for our souls. In fact, hope reaches behind the curtain and into the most holy place. (20) Jesus has gone there ahead of us, and He is our High Priest forever, just like Melchizedek.*

Everything that surrounds us is temporary and there is no safety in anything. In Christ, however, we are like ships anchored safely in port. The anchor gives us safety and stability, especially since we are anchored in the presence of God. For this reason, as Hebrews 10:23 says:

> *Let us hold fast the profession of our faith without wavering; (for he is faithful that promised).*

We must **never** give up.

6. The sword of the Spirit: The sword, the Word of God, has a double purpose in our lives. The sword not only protects us, it also helps us in the offensive by making the devil flee. Hebrews 4:12 says:

For the word of God is quick, and powerful, and sharper than any two-edged sword, piercing even to the dividing asunder of soul and spirit, and of the joints and marrow and is a discerner of the thoughts and intents of the heart.

In Matthew 4:11, Jesus used the expression "It is written" to rebuke the devil. The Greek word used in this place is "rhema", which carries the implication of speaking it in a loud voice. The spoken Word of God is the Sword of the Spirit. When the enemy attacks us with negative thoughts or when he tries to put us in difficult situations where we could fail the Lord, let us answer without hesitation by quoting the Word and saying, "Satan, it is written:

Nay, in all these things we are more than conquerors through him that loved us."
Romans 8:37

My Brothers and Sisters, always remember that the armor covers everything except the back. For this reason, the Roman legions fought in very tight rows (falanges). The soldiers were trained never to break the lines and to protect every other soldier around them. That way, everyone felt confident that he was not fighting alone. We as Christians should not have to fight alone against the enemy. For this reason, it is important that we assemble ourselves and find our place in the body of Christ. It is also important that we cover each other's back.

Unfortunately, many times the one who is supposed to protect us is the person who hurts us. This should not be so, but it happens, so we need to trust that the Lord will place people by our side who will help us and protect us. Let us make the decision to cover one another's back. It is important to note that if the soldier would turn around and run away from the battle, his back would remain unprotected. This could cost him his life. Never turn your back and leave the Gospel. It could cost you your life.

CHAPTER 6
PREPARING FOR BATTLE

Be sober, be vigilant; because your adversary the devil, as a roaring lion, walketh about seeking whom he may devour.
1 Peter 5:8

There are certain things that we as soldiers need to learn about the spiritual battle before we can really be effective in the army of the Lord. Let us examine them:

1. We must learn that our battle is not against each other, but against Satan. In 2 Corinthians 2:11 we read:

Lest Satan should get an advantage of us: for we are not ignorant of his devices.

Ephesians 6:12 adds this:

For we wrestle not against flesh and blood, but against principalities, against powers, against the rulers of the darkness of this world, against the spiritual wickedness in high places.

2. The spiritual battle is a battle for our faith. We can see this clearly in 1 Timothy 6:12 where it reads:

Fight the good fight of faith, lay hold on eternal life, whereunto thou art also called and hast professed a good profession before many witnesses.

3. Jesus has to be our Commander. Hebrews 2:10 states:

For it became him, for whom are all things, and by whom areall things, in bringing many sons unto glory, to make the captain of their salvation perfect through sufferings.

4. We have to fight our battle under the banner of the Lord and with faith. Let us read what the Bible says in Psalm 60:4:

Thou hast given a banner to them that fear thee, that it may be displayed because of the truth. Selah

and in 1 Corinthians 16:13 (Contemporary English Version):

Keep alert. Be firm in your faith. Stay brave and strong.

5. Prayer warriors must be committed. As it is written in 2 Timothy 2:1-4 (Contemporary English Version):

Timothy, my child, Christ Jesus is kind, and you must let him make you strong. (2) You have often heard me teach. Now I want you to tell these same things to followers who can be trusted to tell others. (3) As a good soldier of Christ Jesus you must endure your share of suffering. (4) Soldiers on duty don't work at outside jobs. They try only to please their commanding officer.

Committed soldiers for Christ get involved in the study of the Word. It is through the Word that we can recognize the power of the enemy, and more importantly, of course, the power of God. Trained soldiers know how to pay the price for the victory and do not ignore the wiles of the enemy.

6. A good soldier is not afraid. The enemy can try to intimidate us. We need to know that fear is not of God and that it is an indication that we lack faith. 2 Timothy 1:7 states this:

For God hath not given us the spirit of fear; but of power; and of love, and of a sound mind.

Demons try to infiltrate our mind through intimidation and fear.

7. We must understand that our strength comes from God. Let us read 1 John 4:4 (Contemporary English Version):

Children, you belong to God, and you have defeated these enemies. God's Spirit is in you and is more powerful than the one that is in the world.

The soldier that has a knowledge of spiritual things knows that God is more powerful than the enemy. Those who do not are not effective soldiers.

8. We have to see Satan as someone who has been defeated already. The Bible says:

Nay in all these things we are more than conquerors through him that loved us. (Romans 8:37).

Yes, we are more than conquerors because Christ defeated Satan at Calvary.

9. We have to be careful not to fall into any of his traps. The two most effective traps that the enemy uses against us are spiritual pride and underestimating him.

    a. Spiritual pride: As we experience the victories in our lives we can fall into the trap of thinking that it is because of our spiritual strength and dedication to the Lord that we are defeating the enemy. If we go to battle and think that God will give us His power without humility on our part, we are in trouble. Paul tells us in 1 Corinthians 2:3 (Contemporary English Version):

    At first, I was weak and trembling with fear.

    He explains it better in 2 Corinthians 12:10 (Contemporary English Version):

    Yes, I am glad to be weak or insulted or mistreated or to have troubles and sufferings, if it is for Christ. Because when I am weak, I am strong.

    We can easily think that our victories are due to our own merits, forgetting that it is the Lord who gives us our victories. If we think incorrectly, the enemy will take advantage of us. This is why the Bible clearly teaches us in John 15:4-5 (Contemporary English Version):

    Stay joined to me, and I will stay joined to you. Just as a branch cannot produce fruit unless it stays joined to the vine, you cannot produce fruit unless you stay joined to me.

(5) I am the vine, and you are the branches. If you stay joined to me, and I stay joined to you, then you will produce lots of fruit. But you cannot do anything without me.

b. Underestimating our enemy: A man from Germany named Johanes Fascius took a group of intercessors to the Lenin mausoleum in Moscow. There, they felt led to call on judgement upon the "gods of the Soviet government". I don't know what happened in the spiritual realm, but shortly after their pronouncing that prayer, communism fell. Soon after that, however, Fascius suffered a heart attack, lost all his strength, and almost died. When he recovered, he entered into a severe depression that lasted for three years. It was not until he recognized what was going on that he was delivered. It took a prayer that only lasted 30 seconds. What he experienced was a counter-attack from the spirit of death that they had defeated in the mausoleum (This information was taken from a British magazine). Definitely, we cannot underestimate our enemy.

10. Our teachings about spiritual warfare must be Biblical. How sad it is when you see people talking about exorcisms and getting their teachings or theories from Hollywood. There is only one reality, and that reality is that you can only fight a spiritual battle in the Name of Jesus. This is clearly shown in Romans 14:1:

For it is written, As I live, saith the Lord, every knee shall bow to me, and every tongue shall confess to God.

11. The spiritual battle cannot be ritualistic. In order to be effective you need to have an intimate relationship with the Lord and be dedicated totally to Him. At the same time, the spiritual battle must be accompanied by a sincere desire that souls would be saved and that they would be able to fulfill the plan of God in their lives. A story in the Bible tells about some men who wanted to take advantage of the deliverance ministry and profit from it. We can read this story in Acts 19:13-17 (Contemporary English Version):

Some Jewish men started going around trying to force out evil spirits by using the name of the Lord Jesus. They said to the spirits, "Come out in the name of that same Jesus that Paul preaches about!" (14)Seven sons of a Jewish high priest named Sceva were doing this, (15) when an evil spirit said to them, "I know Jesus! And I have heard about Paul. But who are you?" (16) Then the man with the evil spirit jumped on them and beat them up. They ran out of the house, naked and bruised. (17) When the Jews and Gentiles in Ephesus heard about this, they were so frightened that they praised the name of the Lord Jesus.

12. God desires that every intercessor be under a spiritual covering (a church or ministry). There should not be any "Lone Rangers" for the Lord. Every intercessor should be a member of a local church ministry. God established His church and through His church, He changed the world. He has appointed pastors to take care of the souls. We can read this in Hebrews 13:7:

Remember them which have the rule over you, who have spoken unto you the word of God: whose faith follow considering the end of their conversation.

Intercessors should be submitted to their pastor and inform him of their desire to join the church's intercessory team.

13. Never forget the power of prayer. God has angels to help us in the spiritual battle. Several years ago my son Jann had a vision. He saw a great battle between an angel and a demon that was taking place on our church property. It was a ferocious battle. Every time that the angel would strike the demon, the demon would multiply itself. As Jann watched, he felt that he needed to pray. As he did so, he saw a gigantic hand come from the clouds and destroy the demon. Definitely, God intervenes when we pray fulfilling what the Word says in James 5:16:

Confess your faults one to another and pray one for another that ye may be healed. The effectual fervent prayer of a righteous man availeth much.

When we pray, God sends angels to help us. Prayer gives us the additional push that we need to obtain our victory. Prayer surpasses the kingdom of Satan as God intervenes in a supernatural way. My Brothers and Sisters, we have to be honest when we pray. God does not like vain repetitions. Definitely, lack of prayer can cause a disaster in our spiritual battle.

CHAPTER 7
TRAINING FOR THE BATTLE

Ask, and it shall be given you; seek, and ye shall find; knock, and it shall be opened unto you: (8) For every one that asketh receiveth; and he that seeketh findeth; and to him that knocketh it shall be opened. (9) Or what man is there of you, whom if his son ask bread will he give him a stone? (10) Or if he ask a fish, will he give him a serpent? (11) If ye then, being evil, know how to give good gifts unto your children, how much more shall your Father which is in heaven give good things to them that ask him?
Matthew 7: 7-11

God is the source of all power. Psalm 62:11 says:

God hath spoken once; twice have I heard His; that power belongeth unto God.

If we exercise our authority in Christ, Satan has to change his plans; however, as every good soldier should know, we must be trained to fight the spiritual battle. James 4:7-10 gives us the following instructions:

Submit yourselves therefore to God. Resist the devil, and he will flee from you. (8) Draw nigh to God and he will draw nigh to you, Cleanse your hands, ye sinners; and purify your hearts, ye double minded. (9) Be aflicted, and mourn, and weep: let your laughter be turned to mourning, and your joy to heaviness. (10) Humble yourselves in the sight of the Lord, and He shall lift you up.

There are several things that we may consider from these passages:

1. Verse 7 clearly states that before we can fight the spiritual battle and be victorious, we need to submit to God. To resist implies that our prayer life must be focused on God and His will. We cannot be distracted from our goal, even if, at first, we do not see an answer. Many demons are stubborn. They will test our faith to see if we really believe God's Word and if we really believe that He has authority over them.

2. Verse 8 teaches us that a prayer warrior must live a holy life in submission to the Lord. Isaiah 45:11-13 adds the following:

Thus saith the Lord, the Holy One of Israel, and his Maker, Ask me of things to come concerning my sons, and concerning the worry my hands command ye me. (12) I have made the earth, and created man upon it: I, even my hands, have stretched out the heavens, and all their host have I commanded, (13) I have raised him up in righteousness, and I will direct all his ways: he shall build my city and he shall let go my captives, not for price nor reward, saith the Lord of hosts.

3. In James 4: 9 & 10, the following is implied:

    a. We need to have a strong conviction about the injustices made by the powers of darkness.

    b, We need to be emotionally and spiritually involved with God.

c. We have to discern what our circumstances are, know what is right or wrong, and pray to be victorious.

d. We need to believe the Word and believe that God is able to do more than what we can ask for or think. (Ephesians 3:20). After all, there is nothing impossible for him who believes (Mark 9:23).

Jesus's power and authority are so great that even nature is subject to Him. We can see this when He blessed the bread and the fish and they were multiplied, and when He gave the order and Lazarus was resurrected. We can also see that demons had to submit to His authority. When He ordered the demons to leave a person, the demons left immediately. Brothers and Sisters, Jesus delegated to us His power and authority. He says in John 14:12:

Verily verily I say unto you, He that believeth on me, the works that I do shall he do also; and greater works than these shall he do; because I go unto my Father.

In Matthew 21:21, He repeats it:

Jesus answered and said unto them, Verily I say unto you, If ye have faith, and doubt not, ye shall not only do this which is done to the fig tree, but also if ye shall say unto this mountain, be thou removed and be thou cast into the sea; it shall be done.

Yes, Christ has given us of His power and authority so that we can win. In spiritual warfare we need to know that in Jesus we are more that conquerors. I want to strongly remind you that we will be victorious only if we are submitted to Him and obey His Word.

For the word of God is quick, and powerful, and sharper than any two-edged sword, piercing even to the dividing asunder of soul and spirit, and of the joints and marrow, and is a discerner of the thoughts and intents of the heart.
(Hebrews 4:12).

Wherefore lay apart all filthiness and superfluity of naughtiness, and receive with meekness the engrafted word, which is able to save your souls. (22) But be ye doers of the word, and not hearers only deceiving your own selves. (23) For if any be a hearer of the word, and not a doer he is like unto a man beholding his natural face in a glass: (24) For he beholdeth himself and goeth his way and straight way forgetteth what manner of a man he was.
(James 1:21-24)

4. In verses 19-23 we are presented with God's sovereignty, a theological term that relates to the unlimited power that God possesses. In other words, God has power over everything. The Bible declares that God is fulfilling His redemptive plan through the whole world and nobody can stop Him. He established this plan immediately after the fall of mankind. We see it in Genesis 3:15.

And I will put enmity between thee and the woman, and between thy seed and her seed; it shall bruise thy head, and thou shalt bruise his heel.

This plan was fulfilled at Calvary when Jesus died on the cross. Without that sacrifice, neither freedom nor hope would be available for mankind.

If we read chapter 1 of the book of Ephesians, we see that in verses 6-9 it says:

To the praise of the glory of his grace, wherein he hath made us accepted in the beloved. (7) In whom we have redemption through his blood, the forgiveness of sins, according to the riches of his grace; (8) Wherein he hath abounded toward us in all wisdom and prudence; (9) Having made known unto us the mystery of his will, according to his good pleasure which he hath purposed in himself.

5. We have to be convinced that according to verses 21-23, Jesus has authority over:

"all principality and power, and might, and dominion, and every name that is named, not only in this world, but also in that which is to come: (22) And (God the Father) hath put all things under his feet, and gave him (Jesus) to be the head over all things to the church, (23) Which is his body the fulness of him that filleth all in all."

Here we are told of the omnipotence of God (He can do anything), the omnipresence of God (He is everywhere) and of the omniscience of God (God knows everything).

His power is above all, His name is above all names, and His love is the greatest. Jesus is the King of kings and Lord of lords, as it is stated in Philippians 2:9-11:

Wherefore God also hath highly exalted him, and given him a name which is above every name: That at the name of Jesus every knee should bow of things in heaven, and things in earth, and things under the earth; And that every tongue should confess that Jesus Christ is Lord for the glory of God the Father.

6. Lastly, we need to be convinced of what we are told in Revelations 11:15:

And the seventh angel sounded; and there were great voices in heaven, saying, The kingdoms of this world are become the kingdoms of our Lord, and of his Christ; and he shall reign for ever and ever.

Yes, my Brothers and Sisters, Jesus Christ is the Winner!

CHAPTER 8
THE OFFENSIVE

As it is written, For thy sake we are killed all the day long; we are accounted as sheep for the slaughter (37) Nay in all these things we are more than conquerors through him that loved us. (38) For I am persuaded, that neither death, nor life, nor angels, nor principalities, nor powers, nor things present, nor things to come, (39) Nor height nor depth, nor any other creature, shall be able to separate us from the love of God, which is in Christ Jesus our Lord.
Romans 8:36-39

No war is won unless we advance on the battlefield. A city that is surrounded and besieged eventually loses its desire to fight, and the sense of defeat starts from within. For this reason, it is necessary to develop the offensive. This plan must be agressive and feasible. The main problem with the spiritual battle is that we cannot see the enemy nor our progress. The enemy attacks hard and obstinately. This is why we need to protect ourselves with the shield of faith, trusting that the sword of the Spirit is doing its job and bringing us closer to our victory. Every soldier has to be able to receive and follow his commander's instructions. The way we receive our marching orders is through prayer and through the reading of the Word. When Christians discipline themselves by praying the Biblical way; that is, they are persistent, consistent, and live by faith, they have the strength and the knowledge to overcome.

These people are the prayer warriors who know they have the victory in their hands. The world, however, can only see this victory when Christians show it to them. If we are prayer warriors, our mission should be to manifest to the world that we are victorious, and that Christ, our Commander-in-Chief, has already defeated Satan. Jesus has given us as Christians authority over the principalities and powers of darkness. This authority only works if we use it. We have to be careful, however, to understand that without the Lord we cannot do anything. For this reason, we have to make sure that we are not careless and fall in the trap of the enemy by either having "spiritual pride" or "underestimating our enemy."

Taking this into consideration, if we read Matthew 16:18, we find the following:

And I say also unto thee, that thou art Peter and upon this rock I will build my church; and the gates of hell shall not prevail against it.

Here we are introduced to the term "the gates of hell". Many Christians understand this verse as if the Lord were saying that He will not allow the church to be defeated and that we can count on His protection. This is true, but in reality, this term describes our offensive mode rather than our defensive mode. The world is in darkness and it is up to us Christians to come out of our four walls and rescue the lost from an eternity in hell. We can do this through our preaching and our testimony. This verse assures us that if we use the authority delegated to us by Jesus and if we live according to the Word, God Himself will bring people to salvation and deliver them from darkness into light, or from hell into God's camp.

When a sinner comes to Christ, he becomes a child of God. God has many things for His children. Some examples of His promises are written in John 1:29; 1 Corinthians 15:3, and Colossians 1:14, where God promises that He will cleanse us from all sin. In Revelation 5:12,13 and Acts 1:8; 2:38, He promises the Baptism of the Holy Ghost. These and many other promises are the ones He has prepared for His children. The devil (the enemy) wants to steal them from us. We see this in John 10:10:

> *The thief cometh not, but for to steal, and to kill, and to destroy.*

Praise God, Jesus completes the statement by saying:

> *I am come that they might have life, and that they might have it more abundantly.*

We have to come out of our camp. With the authority that Christ has given us and trusting in His protection, we need to proclaim the Good News of Salvation to others. By proclaiming the Gospel, we can rescue the unsaved from hell, so that they, like us, can have everlasting life with God. This is where the promise that *"the gates of hell shall not prevail"* comes to pass. There is no devil that can prevent people from getting saved. The promises of God are for His people, for those who have accepted Jesus as their personal Savior; however, all of God's promises are conditional to the obedience of His Word. In order to have His promises fulfilled, we need to cleanse our lives (Galatians 5:15; 1 Peter 2:11), and take care of our salvation with fear and trembling (Philippians 2:12). If we do this, not only will we be saved, we will not lose our sensitivity to the things of God. The power of God will help us to defeat the devil and to resist any temptation. Remember Phillipians 4:13.

I can do all things through Christ which strengtheneth me.

Even though many times we see only our problems and battles, God wants us to share the Gospel with others. Isaiah 55:8 says the following:

For my thoughts are not your thoughts, neither are your ways my ways, saith the LORD.

In our human nature, we get tired, and in the flesh, we only think about surviving the trials. We forget that Galatians 5:24 says:

And they that are Christ's, have crucified the flesh with the affections and lusts.

I want to emphasize strongly that God wants us to be witnesses of His power and of the transformation He has done in us. For this reason, we need to guard our testimony, as it is written in 1 Thesalonians 5:22:

Abstain from all appearance of evil.

I repeat, God wants for us, not only to be on the defensive, but to take the offensive in rescuing souls. At the end, the army that wins is not the one who is on the defensive, it is the one that moves forward and overcomes the enemy. In other words, we have the armor of God that protects us from the enemy, but this is only part of what God wants for us. He also wants to protect us when we start our offensive and start rescuing the lost.

CHAPTER 9
WHAT WEAPONS DO WE NEED IN ORDER TO TAKE THE OFFENSIVE?

For the weapons of our warfare are not carnal but mighty in God for pulling down strongholds.
2 Corinthians 10:4

We need to recognize that God equips us, protects us, and gives us the weapons for our offensive. Among those weapons are prayer, praise, our preaching, and our testimony. Let us try to examine them individually.

1. Prayer
Prayer is one of the most powerful weapons we can use in battle. The Bible tells us in 2 Corinthians 10:4:

For the weapons of our warfare are not carnal but mighty in God for pulling down strongholds.

Ephesians 6:18 also states:

Praying always with all prayer and supplication in the Spirit, being watchful to this end with all perseverance and supplication for all the saints.

As you can see, prayer is a very powerful weapon. God miraculously intervenes when we pray. We can see an example of this when Peter was placed in prison and bound to two guards. The story is in Acts 12:5-11 and goes like this:

Peter was therefore kept in prison, but constant prayer was offered to God for him by the church. (6) And when Herod was about to bring him out, that night Peter was sleeping, bound with two chains between two soldiers; and the guards before the door were keeping the prison. (7) Now behold, an angel of the Lord stood by him, and a light shone in the prison; and he struck Peter on the side and raised him up, saying, "Arise quickly". And his chains fell off his hands. (8) Then the angel said to him, "Gird yourself and tie on your sandals"; and so he did. And he said to him, "Put on your garment and follow me. (9) So he went out and followed him, and did not know that what was done by the angel was real, but thought he was seeing a vision. (10) When they were past the first and the second guard posts, they came to the iron gate that leads to the city which opened to them of its own accord; and they went out and went down one street, and immediately the angel departed from him. (11) And when Peter had come to himself he said, "Now I know for certain that the Lord has sent His angel, and has delivered me from the hand of Herod and from all the expectation of the Jewish people."

God intervened and sent an angel to free Peter from prison. In order for anybody to understand the depth of intercessory prayer, the person has to prepare himself. Every soldier has to be trained before going to war. Remember, our battle is against the powers of darkness and this battle is very real and hard. The only way to be victorious is to keep ourselves strong in the Lord. Paul, in Ephesians 6, says that we need to pray in the Spirit. We cannot stop praying. If we stop praying and become slack, we might be wounded and even turn away from the Lord. Then the enemy comes in and works in our mind making it harder to come back spiritually, Taking this fact into consideration, now, more than ever, we need to pray one for another and be always ready for battle,

2. The weapon of praise

Besides prayer, another weapon that we have is praise. Praise makes God manifest Himself supernaturally. It is also the right thing to do when God shows His power. In Exodus 15:9-11, we see this:

The enemy said, "I will pursue, I will overtake, I will divide the spoil; My desire shall be satisfied on them. I will draw my sword, My hand shall destroy them; (10) You blew with your wind, The sea covered them; They sank like lead in the mighty waters. (11) "Who is like You, o Lord, among the gods? Who is like You, glorious in holiness, Fearful in praises, doing wonders?

In these verses, the psalmist praises God for what He has done. Definitely, God is worthy to be praised!

Psalm 22:23:

You who fear the LORD, praise Him! All you descendants of Jacob, glorify Him, And fear Him, all you offspring of Israel!

Revelations 12:10:

Then I heard a loud voice saying in heaven, "Now salvation, and strength, and the kingdom of our God, and the power of His Christ have come, for the accuser of our brethren, who accused them before our God day and night, has been cast down."

Revelations 16:13-14:

And I saw three unclean spirits like frogs coming out of the mouth of the dragon, out of the mouth of the beast, and out of the mouth of the false prophet. (14) For they are spirits of demons, performing signs, which go out to the kings of the earth and of the whole world, to gather them to the battle of that great day of God Almighty.

Psalms 149:6-9:

Let the high praises of God be in their mouth, And a two-edged sword in their hand, (7) To execute vengeance on the nations, And punishments on the peoples; (8) To bind their kings with chains, And their nobles with fetters of iron; (9) To execute on them the written judgment. This honor have all His saints. The Glory will be for His saints, Hallelujah.

1 Corinthians 5:2-3:

And you are puffed up, and have not rather mourned, that he who has done this deed might be taken away from among you. (3) For I indeed, as absent in body but present in spirit, have already judged (as though I were present) him who has so done this deed.

Through the Word of God and the weapon of praise, God gives us the authority to judge kings and rulers of the nations. This is a mighty and wonderful privilege. Also, God moves in the praises of His people. I have found out that when people are disappointed and feel that they are losing their strength, if they start to praise God, strength and joy returns and the victory becomes more evident. Praising God when you are in trials or in battle pleases God. In reality, we are telling Him that we trust Him for the victory even before we see it. It is a demonstration of faith and results in our victory. God honors those who honor Him (1 Samuel 2:30).

3. The weapon of our preaching
Preaching is speaking the Word of God with boldness. The Word is what gives us authority over the enemy. If people do not know the Word of God, they can easily be deceived. In 2 Timothy 4:1-4: God, using the Apostle Paul, says the following:

I charge you therefore before God and the Lord Jesus Christ, who will judge the living and the dead at His appearing and His kingdom; (2) Preach the word! Be ready in season and out of season. Convince, rebuke, exhort, with all longsuffering and teaching. (3) For the time will came when they will not endure sound doctrine, but according to their own desires, because they have itching ears, they will heap up for themselves teachers; (4) and they will turn their ears away from the truth, and be turned aside to fables.
(New King james Version)

Isaiah 55:11 also tells us:

So shall My word be that goes forth from My mouth; It shall not return to Me void, But it shall accomplish what I please, And it shall prosper in the thing for which I sent it.

Hebrews 4:12 states this:

For the word of God is living and powerful, and sharper than any two-edged sword, piercing even to the division of soul and spirit, and of joints and marrow and is a discerner of the thoughts and intents of the heart.

Luke 21:33 adds the promise:

Heaven and earth will pass away but My words will by no means pass away.

As you see, we need to preach all of the Word of God, not leaving anything out. This way, we not only have the backing of the Lord, we will be providing weapons so that others may also obtain their victory.

4. The weapon of our testimony

Acts 1:8 tells us:

But you shall receive power when the Holy Spirit has came upon you; and you shall be witnesses to Me in Jerusalem, and in all Judea and Samaria, and to the ends of the earth.

Revelations 12:7-11:

> And war broke out in heaven: Michael and his angels fought with the dragon; and the dragon and his angels fought (8) but they did not prevail, nor was a place found for them in heaven any longer. (9) So the great dragon was cast out, that serpent of old, called the Devil and Satan, who deceives the whole world; he was cast to the earth, and his angels were cast out with him. (10) Then I heard a loud voice saying in heaven, "Now salvation, and strength, and the kingdom of our God, and the power of His Christ have come, for the accuser of our brethren, who accused them before our God day and night, has been cast down.
> (11) And they overcame him by the blood of the Lamb and by the word of their testimony and they did not love their lives to the death."

Conclusion

We have to be convinced that we are in a battle, that this is a real battle; and that our enemy is not a human being, but the devil and all of his demons. We need to know that we are on the winning side, the side of our Lord Jesus Christ, and take advantage of the fact that God has given us the instructions, the protection, and the necessary weapons to obtain our victory. If we do this, we are more than conquerors. If we use the weapons that God has given us, we will have victory in all of our battles. For this reason, I exhort you to remain faithful to the Lord and to avoid spiritual pride and indifference. Of great importance also is the fact that we cannot underestimate our enemy. If we follow these instructions, then we will not only be firm and victorious until Jesus comes, we will also help others obtain their victory. May God bless you.

About the Author:

Dr. Joffre P Vivoni, a dentist by profession, was called to full-time ministry in 1977. In 1981, he and his family moved from Puerto Rico to the city of Jacksonville, Florida, where he started the Jacksonville Hispanic Church of God and Cross-Cultural Center. He has been a member of both the state and national Cross-Cultural Boards of the Church of God denomination. He has overseen more than 35 Hispanic churches in Florida. He is the president of Southeastern Theological Seminary and of Bible Foundations Center Mission, Inc. He is currently a member of various boards, among them the Church of God Association of Christian Schools, the Florida Council of Private Colleges and the American Council of Private Colleges. Dr. Vivoni is also a charter member of the American Association of Christian Counselors.

Dr. Vivoni has been married to his wife Elia for 32 years. He has three children: two daughters, Laura Caresse Vivoni-Toro and Eliane Marie Smith, and a son, Jann Pascal Vivoni.

He also has three beautiful granddaughters: Gaby, Elsie and Ciara.

Dr. Vivoni's passion is to teach the Word of God.

www.ingramcontent.com/pod-product-compliance
Lightning Source LLC
Chambersburg PA
CBHW060427050426
42449CB00009B/2180